MACARONS, COOKIES, BARS
& Biscotti

METRO BOOKS
New York

An Imprint of Sterling Publishing
387 Park Avenue South
New York, NY 10016

METRO BOOKS and the distinctive Metro Books logo
are trademarks of Sterling Publishing Co., Inc.

© 2013 by ACP Magazines Ltd.

This 2013 edition published by Metro Books by arrangement with ACP Magazines Ltd.

ISBN 978-1-4351-4562-7

For information about custom editions, special sales, and premium and corporate purchases,
please contact Sterling Special Sales at 800-805-5489 or specialsales@sterlingpublishing.com.

Printed in China

2 4 6 8 10 9 7 5 3 1

www.sterlingpublishing.com

MACARONS, COOKIES, BARS & *Biscotti*

Ⓜ
METRO BOOKS
New York

CONTENTS

PERFECT PREPARATION

EQUIPMENT

Bake macarons, cookies, meringues and biscotti on flat oven trays with tiny sides.

• If the sides are over ½ inch high, baking and browning of the cookies will be inadequate and/or uneven. It's better to use the base of an upturned cake pan rather than a high-sided tray.

• Some non-stick oven trays cause cookies to burn on the bottom; reduce the oven temperature to stop this. Do a test run on new tray.

• Rectangular pans vary in size, quality, depth and finishes and can have straight or sloping sides. There's not much difference in their capacities. If the pan is quite full of mixture, the slice will take longer to bake than if the mixture is spread more thinly.

• Know your oven well; make notes of the baking times and temperatures on the recipes. Most domestic ovens have hot spots, so turn pans around during baking. Start checking after a third of the baking time, you might have to turn trays several times for even baking and browning. If you're using two or three racks, switch positions of trays around.

• You'll also need an electric mixer, wooden spoons, plastic or rubber spatulas, a metal spatula, mixing bowls, fine wire racks and a sifter.

PREPARING

You should always read every recipe right through before you start to do anything.

• Preparing all the ingredients before you start to mix is best, unless there are cooling or standing times involved, which would give you time to prepare the rest of the recipe.

• Check and adjust shelf positions in the oven before preheating the oven to the correct temperature. If you're unsure about the accuracy of the oven have its thermostat checked (you can do it yourself by leaving an oven thermometer in the oven so you can easily check).

• Non-stick pans usually need greasing; mostly a light coating of a cooking-oil spray is enough. If the pan is old or scratched use a heavier coating of spray, or grease with butter. Don't over-grease the trays; excess greasing will attract the heat of the oven and may burn the bottoms of the cookies and anywhere, such as the corners of the trays, that isn't covered by cookies.

• Parchment paper can be used instead of greasing, but the paper tends to roll up; a light spray of cooking oil will hold it in position. If we suggest using parchment paper, then it's for a good reason; often parchment paper can be used more than once.

MEASURING

Use the correct measuring spoons and cups for dry ingredients and jugs for liquids.

• Use the blade of a knife or metal spatula to level off dry ingredients in cups and spoons.

• Check the ingredient being measured at eye level for accuracy.

• In our recipes we give both cup and weight measurements. If you are using kitchen scales, check them for accuracy using an unopened block of butter.

• Scales are more consistently accurate than cup measures, especially if making a large quantity of cookies.

The food coloring used in the macaron recipes is optional. Omiting it won't change the flavor or texture.

The oven temperatures in this book are for conventional ovens; if you have a convection oven decrease the temperature by 10-20 degrees.

Cookies of all types, shapes and sizes are easy to make, providing you follow the recipes carefully. Here are some extra tips to help you bake perfect batches every time.

MIXING

For best results, the ingredients should be at room temperature, particularly the butter.

• The creaming process means the butter, sugar and egg(s) are beaten together using an electric mixer. Most cookie recipes say "beat until combined"; don't overbeat or the mixture will be too soft and the cookies will spread too much during baking.

• To start, use low/medium speeds for mixing and don't let the mixture change to a lighter color. The main exception is when you're making bars; at times a "light and fluffy" creamed mixture is needed to achieve a lighter texture.

• Macarons and meringues are made by beating egg whites until soft peaks form. The beaters and bowl must be very clean (grease-free); the smallest speck of yolk will prevent the whites from beating to a foamy, soft peak.

• Place egg whites in a deep bowl, beat at medium speed until whites become foamy and start to hold their shape. Increase the speed a little and beat until the whites reach the correct stage.

• Add sugar, a spoonful at a time; beat the mixture until all the sugar is dissolved before adding the next batch. Test for sugar grains by feeling a little of the mix between your fingertips.

TESTING

Use the baking times we suggest as a guide only.

• Baking times are affected by many factors: temperature of the room and ingredients, oven temperature, accurate measuring, the mixing of the ingredients, oven rack and tray positions, the material the oven trays and cake pans are made from, and so on.

• To test cookies, check towards the end of baking time; use the side of your thumb to gently "push" against the side of one cookie on the tray, it should feel soft, if it slides, even slightly, the cookies are done. Remove from the oven then follow cooling instructions.

• Some cookies are cooled on the trays so they crisp from the heat of the trays, or they could be fragile and need time to settle. More solid cookies are cooled on wire racks.

• Meringues and macarons are usually baked slowly; they're done when they feel dry.

• Biscotti are baked twice, once in a log shape, which is cooled and sliced then dried out in the oven.

• Bars that are cake-like can be tested with a skewer. Some bars are a simple single layer of mixture; don't overbake these as they become dry and hard as they cool. They should feel slightly soft while in the oven and will firm as they cool. Most bars cool in the pan.

STORING

Unfilled cookies will keep about a week in an airtight container at room temperature.

• If unfilled cookies soften they can be re-crisped in the oven. Preheat the oven to 350°F. Place cookies in a single layer on an ungreased oven tray; leave in the oven about 5 minutes or until they feel dry. Cool on wire racks.

• Filled cookies soften during storage, but sometimes this makes them better to eat. Most butter, chocolate or cream-based fillings need to be stored in an airtight container in the fridge.

• Cream-filled fragile cookies, like brandy snaps and macarons, should be filled no more than 30 minutes before serving, depending on room temperature.

• Unfilled fragile cookies, like meringues and macarons, can be stored in an airtight container at room temperature about a week.

• Biscotti, once properly dried, will keep for months when stored in an airtight container at a cool room temperature.

• Bars will keep in an airtight container in the fridge or at room temperature, depending on their ingredients, for about a week.

• Cookies (except filled fragile cookies, meringues and macarons) and bars will freeze successfully for at least a month.

Macarons

CHOCOLATE ALMOND MACARONS

3 egg whites
¼ cup superfine sugar
1 cup confectioners' sugar
¼ cup cocoa powder
1 cup ground almonds
2 teaspoons cocoa powder, extra
¼ cup pouring cream
5 ounces semi-sweet chocolate, chopped finely

1 Grease oven trays; line with parchment paper.
2 Beat egg whites in small bowl with electric mixer until soft peaks form. Add superfine sugar, beat until sugar dissolves; transfer mixture to large bowl. Fold in sifted confectioners' sugar and cocoa, and ground almonds, in two batches.
3 Spoon mixture into piping bag fitted with ¾-inch plain tube. Pipe 1½-inch rounds about ¾-inch apart onto trays. Tap trays on bench so macarons spread slightly. Dust macarons with extra sifted cocoa; stand 30 minutes.
4 Meanwhile, preheat oven to 300°F.
5 Bake macarons about 20 minutes. Cool on trays.
6 Bring cream to the boil in small saucepan, remove from heat; add chocolate, stir until smooth. Refrigerate about 20 minutes or until spreadable.
7 Sandwich macarons with chocolate filling.

prep + cook time 40 minutes (+ standing & refrigeration)
makes 16
notes Unfilled macarons will keep in an airtight container for about a week. Fill macarons just before serving.

COCONUT ALMOND MACARONS

3 egg whites
¼ cup superfine sugar
½ teaspoon coconut extract
1¼ cups confectioners' sugar
¾ cup ground almonds
¼ cup desiccated coconut
2 teaspoons confectioners'
  sugar, extra
¼ cup cream
5 ounces white eating
  chocolate, chopped finely
2 teaspoons coconut-flavored
  liqueur

1 Grease oven trays; line with parchment paper.
2 Beat egg whites in small bowl with electric mixer until soft peaks form. Add superfine sugar and extract, beat until sugar dissolves; transfer mixture to large bowl. Fold in sifted confectioner's sugar, ground almonds and coconut, in two batches.
3 Spoon mixture into piping bag fitted with ¾-inch plain tube. Pipe 1½-inch rounds about ¾-inch apart onto trays. Tap trays on bench so macarons spread slightly. Dust macarons with extra sifted icing sugar; stand 30 minutes.
4 Meanwhile, preheat oven to 300°F.

5 Bake macarons about 20 minutes. Cool on trays.
6 Bring cream to the boil in small saucepan, remove from heat; add chocolate, stir until smooth. Stir in liqueur. Refrigerate 20 minutes or until spreadable.
7 Sandwich macarons with chocolate filling.

prep + cook time 40 minutes (+ standing & refrigeration)
makes 16
notes Unfilled macarons will keep in an airtight container for about a week. Fill macarons just before serving.

ORANGE ALMOND MACARONS

3 egg whites
¼ cup superfine sugar
orange food coloring
1¼ cups confectioners' sugar
1 cup ground almonds
1 teaspoon finely grated
   orange rind
2 tablespoons flaked almonds
⅓ cup orange marmalade

1 Grease oven trays; line with parchment paper.
2 Beat egg whites in small bowl with electric mixer until soft peaks form. Add superfine sugar and a few drops of coloring, beat until sugar dissolves; transfer mixture to large bowl. Fold in sifted confectioners' sugar, ground almonds and rind, in two batches.
3 Spoon mixture into piping bag fitted with ¾-inch plain tube. Pipe 1½-inch rounds about ¾-inch apart onto trays. Tap trays on bench so macarons spread slightly. Sprinkle macarons with flaked almonds; stand 30 minutes.
4 Meanwhile, preheat oven to 300°F.
5 Bake macarons about 20 minutes. Cool on trays.
6 Sandwich macarons with marmalade.

prep + cook time 40 minutes (+ standing & cooling)
makes 16
notes Unfilled macarons will keep in an airtight container for about a week. Fill macarons just before serving. If the marmalade is too chunky or thick to spread, warm it, strain it, and leave it to cool before using.

PISTACHIO & ORANGE BLOSSOM MACARONS

⅓ cup unsalted roasted
   pistachios
3 egg whites
¼ cup superfine sugar
green food coloring
1¼ cups confectioners' sugar
¾ cup ground almonds
1 tablespoon confectioners'
   sugar, extra
¼ cup cream
5 ounces white chocolate,
   chopped coarsely
4 teaspoons orange
   blossom water

1 Grease oven trays; line with parchment paper.
2 Process pistachios until ground finely.
3 Beat egg whites in small bowl with electric mixer until soft peaks form. Add superfine sugar and a few drops of coloring, beat until sugar dissolves; transfer mixture to large bowl. Fold in ¼ cup of the ground pistachios, sifted confectioners' sugar and ground almonds, in two batches.
4 Spoon mixture into piping bag fitted with ¾-inch plain tube. Pipe 1½-inch rounds about ¾ inch apart onto trays. Tap trays on counter so macarons spread slightly. Dust macarons with extra sifted confectioners' sugar; sprinkle with remaining ground pistachios. Stand 30 minutes.

5 Meanwhile, preheat oven to 300°F.
6 Bake macarons about 20 minutes. Cool on trays.
7 Bring cream to the boil in small saucepan, remove from heat; add chocolate, stir until smooth. Stir in orange blossom water. Refrigerate until spreadable.
8 Sandwich macarons with white chocolate filling.

prep + cook time 40 minutes
(+ standing & refrigeration)
makes 16
notes Unfilled macarons will keep in an airtight container for about a week. Fill macarons just before serving.

LEMON LIQUEUR MACARONS

3 egg whites
¼ cup superfine sugar
yellow food coloring
1¼ cups confectioners' sugar
1 cup ground almonds
2 teaspoons finely grated
   lemon rind
1 tablespoon confectioners'
   sugar, extra
¼ cup cream
5 ounces white chocolate,
   chopped coarsely
4 teaspoons limoncello liqueur

1 Grease oven trays; line with parchment paper.
2 Beat egg whites in small bowl with electric mixer until soft peaks form. Add superfine sugar and a few drops of coloring, beat until sugar dissolves; transfer mixture to large bowl. Fold in sifted confectioners' sugar, ground almonds and rind, in two batches.
3 Spoon mixture into piping bag fitted with ¾-inch plain tube. Pipe 1½-inch rounds about ¾ inch apart onto trays. Tap trays on counter so macarons spread slightly. Dust macarons with extra sifted icing sugar. Stand 30 minutes.
4 Meanwhile, preheat oven to 300°F.
5 Bake macarons about 20 minutes. Cool on trays.

6 Bring cream to the boil in small saucepan, remove from heat; add chocolate, stir until smooth. Stir in liqueur, stand at room temperature until spreadable.
7 Sandwich macarons with chocolate filling.

prep + cook time 40 minutes (+ standing) **makes** 16
notes Unfilled macarons will keep in an airtight container for about a week. Fill macarons just before serving.

COCONUT MACARONS

2 egg whites
½ cup superfine sugar
1 teaspoon vanilla extract
¼ cup plain (all-purpose) flour
1½ cups desiccated coconut
6 glacé cherries, quartered

1 Preheat oven to 300°F. Grease oven trays; line with parchment paper.
2 Beat egg whites in small bowl with electric mixer until soft peaks form. Gradually add sugar, beating until dissolved between additions. Stir in extract, sifted flour and coconut, in two batches.
3 Drop level tablespoons of the mixture onto trays about 2 inches apart. Place cherry quarter on top of each macaron.
4 Bake macarons about 30 minutes. Cool on trays.

prep + cook time 50 minutes
makes 24
notes Macarons will keep in an airtight container for about a week. Glacé cherries are available in three colors, if they're hard to find use any type of glacé fruit you like.

COCONUT, CRANBERRY & WHITE CHOCOLATE MACARONS

2 egg whites
½ cup superfine sugar
1 teaspoon vanilla extract
¼ cup plain (all-purpose) flour
1½ cups desiccated coconut
⅓ cup dried cranberries,
    chopped coarsely
3 ounces white eating
    chocolate, chopped finely
28 whole dried cranberries

1 Preheat oven to 300°F. Grease oven trays; line with parchment paper.
2 Beat egg whites in small bowl with electric mixer until soft peaks form. Gradually add sugar, beating until dissolved after each addition. Stir in extract, sifted flour, coconut, chopped cranberries and chocolate, in two batches.
3 Using wet hands, roll rounded tablespoons of mixture into balls; place about 2 inches apart onto trays. Press a whole cranberry on each macaron.
4 Bake macarons about 25 minutes; cool on trays.

prep + cook time 50 minutes
makes 28
note Macarons will keep in an airtight container for about a week.

CARAMEL PECAN MACARONS

1⅔ cups pecans
2 egg whites
½ cup firmly packed light brown
  sugar
1 teaspoon vanilla extract
¼ cup plain (all-purpose) flour
22 pecan halves

1 Preheat oven to 300°F.
Grease oven trays; line with
parchment paper.
2 Blend or process pecans until
ground finely.
3 Beat egg whites and sugar
in small bowl with electric mixer
about 15 minutes or until sugar
is dissolved. Stir in extract,
sifted flour and ground pecans,
in two batches.
4 Drop rounded tablespoons
of mixture 2 inches apart onto
trays. Press one nut on top of
each macaron.
5 Bake macarons about
30 minutes; cool on trays.

prep + cook time 55 minutes
makes 22
note Macarons will keep in
an airtight container for about
a week.

DARK CHOCOLATE & WALNUT MACARONS

2 cups walnuts
2 egg whites
½ cup superfine sugar
1 teaspoon vanilla extract
1 tablespoon plain
   (all-purpose) flour
4 teaspoons cocoa powder
3 ounces semi-sweet chocolate,
   chopped finely
2 ounces semi-sweet chocolate,
   extra, melted

1 Preheat oven to 300°F. Grease oven trays; line with parchment paper.
2 Blend or process walnuts until ground finely.
3 Beat egg whites in small bowl with electric mixer until soft peaks form. Gradually add sugar, beating until dissolved after each addition. Stir in extract, sifted flour and cocoa, ground walnuts and chopped chocolate, in two batches.
4 Drop rounded tablespoons of mixture 2 inches apart onto trays.
5 Bake macarons about 25 minutes; cool on trays. Drizzle cooled macarons with melted chocolate; stand at room temperature until set.

prep + cook time 1 hour (+ standing) **makes** 24
note Macarons will keep in an airtight container for about a week.

ALMOND MACARONS

2 egg whites
½ cup superfine sugar
1¼ cups ground almonds
½ teaspoon almond extract
¼ cup plain (all-purpose) flour
18 whole blanched almonds

1 Preheat oven to 300°F. Grease oven trays; line with parchment paper.
2 Beat egg whites in small bowl with electric mixer until soft peaks form. Gradually add sugar, beating until dissolved between additions. Fold in ground almonds, extract and sifted flour, in two batches.
3 Drop level tablespoons of mixture about 2 inches apart onto trays. Place one blanched almond on top of each macaron.
4 Bake macarons about 1 hour. Cool on trays.

prep + cook time
1 hour 20 minutes
makes 18
note Macarons will keep in an airtight container for about a week.

HONEY ALMOND MACARONS

2 egg whites
½ cup superfine sugar
1 teaspoon vanilla extract
4 teaspoons honey
¼ cup plain (all-purpose) flour
1 cup ground almonds
1 cup desiccated coconut
¼ cup flaked almonds
1 tablespoon confectioners'
  sugar

1 Preheat oven to 300°F.
Grease oven trays; line with
parchment paper.
2 Beat egg whites in small
bowl with electric mixer until
soft peaks form. Gradually add
superfine sugar, beating until
dissolved after each addition.
Stir in extract, honey, sifted flour,
ground almonds and coconut,
in two batches.
3 Drop level tablespoons of
mixture about 2 inches apart
onto trays. Sprinkle macarons
with flaked almonds.
4 Bake macarons about
45 minutes; cool on trays.
Dust with sifted confectioners'
sugar.

prep + cook time 55 minutes
makes 26
note Macarons will keep in
an airtight container for about
a week.

RASPBERRY MACARONS

3 egg whites
¼ cup superfine sugar
pink food coloring
1¼ cups confectioners' sugar
1 cup ground almonds
1 tablespoon raspberry puree
(see notes)
1 tablespoon confectioners'
sugar, extra
¼ cup pouring cream
5 ounces white chocolate,
chopped coarsely
1 tablespoon raspberry jam,
warmed, sieved

1 Grease oven trays; line with parchment paper.
2 Beat egg whites in small bowl with electric mixer until soft peaks form. Add superfine sugar and a few drops of coloring, beat until sugar dissolves; transfer mixture to large bowl. Fold in sifted confectioners' sugar, ground almonds and raspberry puree, in two batches.
3 Spoon mixture into piping bag fitted with ¾-inch plain tube. Pipe 1½-inch rounds about ¾ inch apart onto trays. Tap trays on bench so macarons spread slightly. Dust macarons with extra sifted confectioners' sugar; stand 30 minutes.
4 Meanwhile, preheat oven to 300°F.
5 Bake macarons about 20 minutes. Cool on trays.

6 Bring cream to the boil in small saucepan, remove from heat; add chocolate, stir until smooth. Stir in jam and a few drops of coloring. Refrigerate until spreadable.
7 Sandwich macarons with chocolate filling.

prep + cook time 40 minutes
(+ standing & refrigeration)
makes 16
notes Push 6 fresh or thawed frozen raspberries through a fine sieve to make raspberry puree. Unfilled macarons will keep in an airtight container for about a week. Fill macarons just before serving.

PLAIN & FILLED
Cookies

CHOCOLATE CHIP COOKIES

8 ounces butter, softened
1 teaspoon vanilla extract
¾ cup superfine sugar
¾ cup firmly packed light brown
  sugar
1 egg
2¼ cups plain (all-purpose) flour
1 teaspoon baking soda
5 ounces dark chocolate melts,
  chopped coarsely

1 Preheat oven to 350°F. Grease oven trays.
2 Beat butter, extract, sugars and egg in small bowl with electric mixer until light and fluffy. Transfer mixture to large bowl; stir in sifted flour and soda, in two batches. Stir in chocolate.
3 Roll tablespoons of mixture into balls; place about 2 inches apart on trays.
4 Bake cookies about 15 minutes; cool on trays.

prep + cook time 30 minutes
makes 36
notes Dark chocolate can be replaced with milk or white chocolate. For choc-nut cookies, replace a third of the chocolate with roasted chopped nuts such as hazelnuts, walnuts, pecans or macadamias. Cookies will keep in an airtight container for up to a week.

ANZAC COOKIES

4 ounces butter, chopped
2 tablespoons golden syrup
   or treacle
1 tablespoon water
½ teaspoon baking soda
1 cup firmly packed light brown
   sugar
½ cup desiccated coconut
1 cup rolled oats
1 cup plain (all-purpose) flour

1 Preheat oven to 325°F. Line oven trays with baking paper.
2 Stir butter, syrup and the water in large saucepan over low heat until smooth. Remove from heat; stir in soda then remaining ingredients.
3 Roll tablespoons of mixture into balls; place about 2 inches apart on trays, then flatten slightly.
4 Bake biscuits about 20 minutes; cool on trays.

prep + cook time 35 minutes
makes 25
notes Biscuits should still feel soft when they're cooked; they will firm up as they cool. Store biscuits in an airtight container for up to a week.

MINI FLORENTINES

¾ cup raisins

2 cups corn flakes

¾ cup roasted flaked almonds

½ cup red glacé cherries

⅔ cup sweetened condensed milk

2 ounces white chocolate, melted

2 ounces semi-sweet chocolate, melted

1 Preheat oven to 350°F. Line oven trays with baking paper.
2 Combine raisins, corn flakes, nuts, cherries and condensed milk in medium bowl.
3 Drop tablespoons of mixture about 2 inches apart on trays.
4 Bake florentines about 5 minutes; cool on trays.
5 Spread the bases of half the florentines with white chocolate; spread remaining florentine bases with dark chocolate. Run fork through chocolate to make waves; stand at room temperature until set.

prep + cook time 25 minutes (+ standing) **makes** 25
note Store florentines in an airtight container in the fridge for up to a week.

HONEY JUMBLES

2 ounces butter
½ cup firmly packed dark brown sugar
¾ cup golden syrup or treacle
1 egg
2½ cups plain (all-purpose) flour
½ cup self-raising flour
½ teaspoon baking soda
2 teaspoons ground ginger
1 teaspoon ground cinnamon
1 teaspoon mixed spice
½ teaspoon ground cloves

glacé icing
1 egg white
1½ cups confectioners' sugar
2 teaspoons plain (all-purpose) flour
1 tablespoon lemon juice, approximately
pink food coloring

1 Preheat oven to 350°F. Grease oven trays.
2 Stir butter, sugar and syrup in medium saucepan, over low heat, until smooth.
3 Transfer mixture to large bowl; cool 10 minutes. Stir in egg then sifted dry ingredients, in two batches. Knead dough on floured surface until dough loses its stickiness, cover; refrigerate 30 minutes.
4 Divide dough into eight portions. Roll each portion into ¾-inch thick sausage; cut each sausage into five 2¼-inch lengths. Place about 1 inch apart on oven trays. Make ends rounded with lightly floured fingers and flatten slightly.
5 Bake jumbles about 15 minutes; cool on trays.
6 Make glacé icing.
7 Spread jumbles with pink and white icing; stand at room temperature until set.

glacé icing Beat egg white lightly in small bowl; gradually stir in sifted confectioners' sugar and flour, then enough juice to make icing spreadable. Place half the mixture in another small bowl; tint with coloring. Keep icings covered with a damp tea towel while in use so they don't dry out.

prep + cook time 40 minutes (+ refrigeration & standing)
makes 40
note Store jumbles in an airtight container for up to a week.

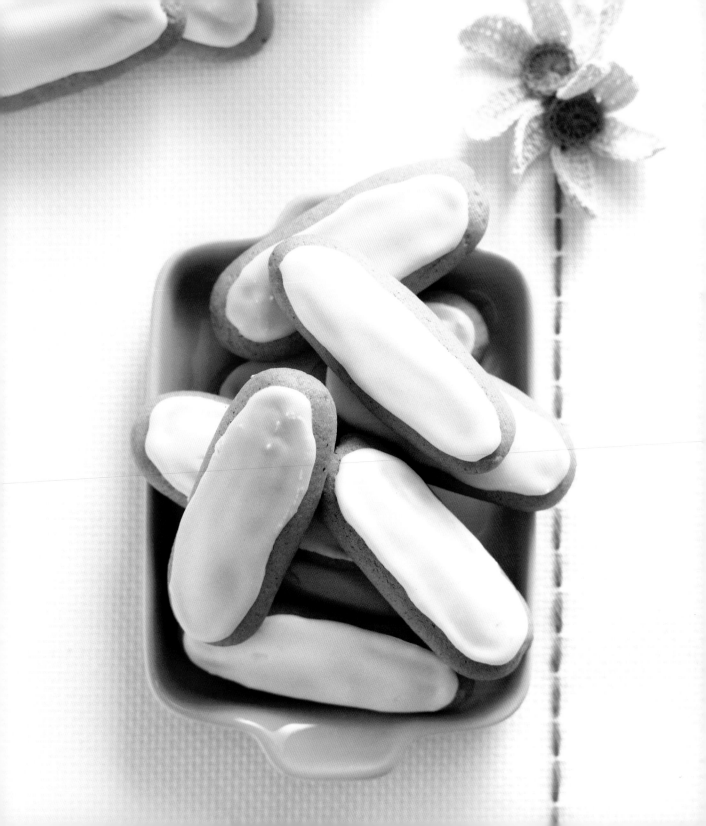

REFRIGERATOR SLICE & BAKE COOKIES

8 ounces butter, softened
1 cup confectioners' sugar
2½ cups plain (all-purpose) flour

1 Beat butter and sifted confectioners' sugar in small bowl with electric mixer until light and fluffy. Transfer to large bowl; stir in sifted flour, in two batches.
2 Knead dough lightly on floured surface until smooth. Divide dough in half; roll each half into a 10-inch log. Enclose dough in plastic wrap; refrigerate about 1 hour or until firm.
3 Preheat oven to 350°F. Grease oven trays.
4 Cut logs into ½-inch slices; place 1 inch apart on trays.
5 Bake cookies about 10 minutes. Cool on trays.

prep + cook time 30 minutes (+ refrigeration) **makes** 50
notes These basic cookies can be topped with nuts before baking or, once cooked, iced then dipped into various sprinkles, or simply dusted lightly with sifted confectioners' sugar. If you want to flavor the dough, beat any essence or extract of your choice with the butter and sugar mixture, or beat in a teaspoon or two of the rind of any finely grated citrus fruit. The cookies will keep in an airtight container for at least a week.

CHOCOLATE CHUNK & RASPBERRY COOKIES

4 ounces butter, softened
¾ cup firmly packed light brown
   sugar
1 egg
1 teaspoon vanilla extract
1 cup plain (all-purpose) flour
¼ cup self-raising flour
⅓ cup cocoa powder
½ teaspoon baking soda
3 ounces semi-sweet chocolate,
   chopped coarsely
4 ounces frozen raspberries

1 Preheat oven to 350°F.
Line oven trays with baking paper.
2 Beat butter, sugar, egg
and extract in small bowl with
electric mixer until combined.
Stir in sifted flours, cocoa and
soda, in two batches, then stir in
chocolate and raspberries.
3 Drop tablespoons of mixture
about 2 inches apart onto trays;
flatten slightly.
4 Bake cookies about 12 minutes.
Stand cookies on trays 5 minutes
before transferring to a wire rack
to cool.

prep + cook time 35 minutes
makes 24
notes Mix and match different
colored chocolates with different
berries if you like. Store cookies
in an airtight container in the
fridge for up to a week.

COCONUT SESAME CRISPS

1 teaspoon honey
¾ ounce butter
1 egg white
2 tablespoons superfine sugar
2 tablespoons plain
  (all-purpose) flour
1 tablespoon desiccated
  coconut
2 teaspoons sesame seeds

1 Stir honey and butter in small saucepan over low heat until smooth; cool.
2 Preheat oven to 325°F. Line two oven trays with parchment paper; mark four 3-inch circles on paper on each tray, turn paper over.
3 Beat egg white in small bowl with electric mixer until soft peaks form; gradually add sugar, beating until dissolved. Fold in sifted flour and butter mixture.
4 Spread level teaspoons of mixture to fill center of each circle on trays; sprinkle with combined coconut and seeds.
5 Bake one tray of crisps at a time about 5 minutes. Remove crisps from tray immediately using metal spatula; place crisps over rolling pin to cool.

prep + cook time 1 hour
makes 28
notes You may find it easier to bake just two crisps on a tray at a time. Re-use the parchment-paper lining. Store crisps in an airtight container for up to a week.

PEANUT CRUNCH COOKIES

¾ cup self-raising flour
¼ teaspoon baking soda
½ teaspoon ground cinnamon
½ cup rolled oats
⅓ cup desiccated coconut
1 teaspoon finely grated
   lemon rind
½ cup crunchy peanut butter
¾ cup superfine sugar
1 tablespoon golden syrup
   or treacle
2 tablespoons cold water,
   approximately

1 Process flour, soda, cinnamon, oats, coconut, rind and peanut butter until crumbly; add sugar, golden syrup and enough of the water to make a firm dough. Knead dough lightly on floured surface until smooth; cover, refrigerate 30 minutes.
2 Preheat oven to 350°F. Grease oven trays.
3 Divide dough in half; roll each half between sheets of parchment paper to ¼-inch thickness. Cut dough into 2¼-inch rounds; place on trays 1 inch apart.
4 Bake cookies about 10 minutes. Stand biscuits on trays 5 minutes before transferring to a wire rack to cool.

prep + cook time 35 minutes (+ refrigeration) **makes** 30
note Store cookies in an airtight container for up to a week.

PEANUT·PRALINE COOKIES

4 ounces butter, softened
¼ cup crunchy peanut butter
½ cup firmly packed light brown
   sugar
1 egg
1½ cups plain (all-purpose) flour
½ teaspoon baking soda
peanut praline
¾ cup roasted unsalted peanuts
½ cup superfine sugar
2 tablespoons water

1 Make peanut praline.
2 Preheat oven to 25°F. Line oven trays with parchment paper.
3 Beat butter, peanut butter, sugar and egg in small bowl with electric mixer until combined. Stir in sifted dry ingredients and half the crushed peanut praline.
4 Roll tablespoons of mixture into balls; place on trays about 2 inches apart, flatten slightly. Sprinkle cookies with remaining praline.
5 Bake cookies about 20 minutes. Cool on trays.

peanut praline Place peanuts on baking-paper-lined oven tray. Combine sugar and the water in small frying pan, stir over heat, without boiling, until sugar is dissolved. Bring to the boil; boil, uncovered, without stirring, until mixture turns a golden brown. Pour mixture over nuts; stand at room temperature until set. Process until coarsely crushed.

prep + cook time 45 minutes (+ standing) **makes** 28
notes Store cookies in an airtight container for up to a week. To save time, you can use 8 ounces purchased peanut brittle instead of the praline.

GINGERBREAD PEOPLE

4 ounces unsalted butter, softened
½ cup firmly packed dark brown sugar
1 egg yolk
2½ cups plain (all-purpose) flour
1 teaspoon baking soda
3 teaspoons ground ginger
½ cup golden syrup
1 tablespoon pink round sprinkles
royal icing
1 egg white
1½ cups confectioners' sugar
4 drops lemon juice
yellow and pink food coloring

1 Preheat oven to 350°F. Line oven trays with parchment paper.
2 Beat butter, sugar and egg yolk in small bowl with electric mixer until smooth; transfer to large bowl. Stir in sifted dry ingredients and syrup, in two batches.
3 Knead dough gently on floured surface until smooth. Divide dough in half; roll each half between sheets of parchment paper to ¼-inch thickness. Cut dough into 6 x 4½-inch girl shapes, 6 x 4½-inch boy shapes and 12 x 2¼-inch flower shapes; place on trays 1 inch apart.
4 Bake gingerbread about 10 minutes. Cool on trays.
5 Meanwhile, make royal icing.
6 Using picture as a guide, pipe icing onto cookies using the three different colors; sprinkle centers of flowers with pink sprinkles. Set at room temperature.

royal icing Beat egg white in small bowl with electric mixer; gradually beat in sifted confectioners' sugar. When mixture reaches piping consistency, beat in juice. Divide icing between three bowls; tint one bowl with yellow coloring and another with pink coloring; leave the remaining bowl plain.

prep + cook time 50 minutes
makes 24
notes Gingerbread can be stored in an airtight container for at least a week. You can cut out any shapes you like from the dough. Be careful not to overcook the shapes, they should still feel soft when they're cooked; they become crisp on cooling.

AMARETTI

1 cup ground almonds
1 cup superfine sugar
2 egg whites
¼ teaspoon almond extract
20 blanched almonds

1 Grease oven trays.
2 Beat ground almonds, sugar, egg whites and extract in small bowl with electric mixer for 3 minutes; stand 5 minutes.
3 Spoon mixture into piping bag fitted with ½-inch plain tube. Pipe mixture onto trays in circular motion, from center out, until about 1½ inches in diameter. Top each amaretti with a nut, cover unbaked amaretti loosely with foil; stand at room temperature overnight (see notes).
4 Preheat oven to 350°F.
5 Bake cookies about 12 minutes. Stand on trays 5 minutes before transferring to a wire rack to cool.

prep + cook time 30 minutes (+ standing) **makes** 20
notes These biscuits are best if the mixture stands overnight: they will work if they're baked straight away, but they're just not quite as good. Amaretti will keep in an airtight container for at least a week.

CHOCOLATE WHEATIES

3 ounces butter, softened
½ cup firmly packed light brown
    sugar
1 egg
¼ cup desiccated coconut
⅓ cup wheat germ
⅔ cup whole wheat plain (all-
    purpose) flour
⅓ cup white self-raising flour
6 ounces semi-sweet chocolate,
    melted

1 Beat butter and sugar in small bowl with electric mixer until smooth; add egg, beat until combined. Stir in coconut, wheat germ and sifted flours.
2 Roll dough between sheets of parchment paper until ¼-inch thick. Place on tray; refrigerate 30 minutes.
3 Preheat oven to 350°F. Line oven trays with parchment paper.
4 Cut 3-inch rounds from dough; place rounds about 1 inch apart on trays.
5 Bake wheaties about 20 minutes. Cool on trays.
6 Spread bases of wheaties with chocolate; mark with a fork. Stand at room temperature until set.

prep + cook time 50 minutes (+ refrigeration & standing)
makes 18
note If the weather is cool, store cookies in an airtight container at room temperature – refrigerate them if the weather is hot.

TRADITIONAL SHORTBREAD

8 ounces butter, softened
⅓ cup superfine sugar
1 tablespoon water
2 cups plain (all-purpose) flour
½ cup rice flour
2 tablespoons white
   (granulated) sugar

1 Preheat oven to 325°F. Grease oven trays.
2 Beat butter and superfine sugar in medium bowl with electric mixer until light and fluffy; stir in the water and sifted flours, in two batches. Knead mixture on floured surface until smooth.
3 Divide mixture in half; shape each half on separate trays into 8-inch rounds. Mark each round into 12 wedges; prick with fork. Pinch edges of rounds with fingers; sprinkle shortbread with white sugar.
4 Bake about 40 minutes; stand 5 minutes. Using sharp knife, cut into wedges along marked lines. Cool on trays.

prep + cook time 1 hour
makes 24
notes Ground white rice can be used instead of rice flour, although it is slightly coarser in texture. Store shortbread in an airtight container for up to a week.

MONTE CARLOS

6 ounces butter, softened
1 teaspoon vanilla extract
½ cup firmly packed light brown
   sugar
1 egg
1¼ cups self-raising flour
¾ cup plain (all-purpose) flour
½ cup desiccated coconut
¼ cup raspberry jam (conserve)
cream filling
2 ounces butter
½ teaspoon vanilla extract
¾ cup confectioners' sugar
2 teaspoons milk

1 Preheat oven to 350°F. Grease oven trays.
2 Beat butter, extract, sugar and egg in small bowl with electric mixer until smooth. Transfer mixture to large bowl, stir in sifted flours and coconut in two batches.
3 Roll rounded teaspoons of mixture into oval shapes; place about 1 inch apart on trays. Flatten slightly; rough surface with fork.
4 Bake cookies about 12 minutes. Cool on wire racks.
5 Make cream filling.
6 Sandwich cookies with jam and filling.

cream filling Beat butter, extract and sifted confectioners' sugar in small bowl with electric mixer until light and fluffy; beat in milk.

prep + cook time 1 hour
makes 25
notes Unfilled cookies will keep in an airtight container for up to a week. Filled cookies will keep for a few days in an airtight container in the fridge.

MELTING MOMENTS

8 ounces butter, softened
1 teaspoon vanilla extract
½ cup confectioners' sugar
1½ cups plain (all-purpose) flour
½ cup cornstarch
butter cream
3 ounces butter
¾ cup confectioners' sugar
1 teaspoon finely grated
  lemon rind
1 teaspoon lemon juice

1 Preheat oven to 325°F. Line oven trays with parchment paper.
2 Beat butter, extract and sifted confectioners' sugar in small bowl with electric mixer until light and fluffy. Transfer mixture to large bowl, stir in sifted flours, in two batches.
3 With floured hands, roll rounded teaspoons of mixture into balls; place about 1 inch apart on trays. Flatten slightly with a floured fork.
4 Bake cookies about 15 minutes. Stand 5 minutes before lifting onto wire racks to cool.
5 Make butter cream.
6 Sandwich cookies with butter cream. Dust with extra sifted confectioners' sugar before serving, if you like.

butter cream Beat butter, sifted confectioners' sugar and rind in small bowl with electric mixer until pale and fluffy; beat in juice.

prep + cook time 40 minutes
makes 25
notes Unfilled cookies will keep in an airtight container for up to a week. Filled cookies will keep for a few days in an airtight container in the fridge.

BRANDY SNAPS

3 ounces butter
½ cup firmly packed dark brown
  sugar
⅓ cup golden syrup or treacle
1 teaspoon ground ginger
⅔ cup plain (all-purpose) flour
1 teaspoon lemon juice
1¼ cups heavy cream (see note),
  whipped

1 Preheat oven to 350°F. Grease oven trays.
2 Stir butter, sugar, syrup and ginger in medium saucepan, over low heat, until smooth. Remove from heat; stir in sifted flour and juice.
3 Drop rounded teaspoons of mixture about 2 inches apart onto trays. Using a wet, thin metal spatula, spread mixture into 3¼-inch rounds.
4 Bake snaps about 8 minutes or until snaps are bubbling and golden brown.
5 Slide a thin metal spatula under each snap; quickly shape each one into a cone. Place snaps on wire rack to cool. Fill with cream just before serving.

prep + cook time 40 minutes
makes 32
notes It is fine to use 10 oz. of heavy cream in this recipe. Brandy is not an ingredient in brandy snaps today, but was possibly included many years ago. If you like, add a little confectioners' sugar and a tablespoon of brandy to the whipped cream. Bake the first tray of snaps and while they are cooking prepare the next tray of snaps; put them into the oven as you're getting the first batch out. If you handle four snaps at a time, the process will be easy. Snaps are best made on the day of serving.

CHOCOLATE CARAMEL SHORTBREAD COOKIES

18 round shortbread cookies
  (see notes)
6 ounces semi-sweet chocolate,
  chopped coarsely
2 teaspoons vegetable oil
caramel filling
½ cup firmly packed
  light brown sugar
2 ounces butter, chopped
2 teaspoons water
1½ tablespoons cornstarch
½ cup milk
1 egg yolk
1 teaspoon vanilla extract

1 Make caramel filling.
2 Spread caramel filling over half of the shortbread cookies; top with remaining cookies. Cover; refrigerate 1 hour.
3 Melt chocolate in small heatproof bowl over saucepan of simmering water (do not allow water to touch base of bowl). Remove from heat; stir in oil.
4 Dip one side of cookies in melted chocolate. Stand at room temperature until set.
caramel filling Stir sugar, butter and the water in small saucepan over heat until sugar is dissolved. Stir in blended cornstarch and milk; stir over heat until mixture boils and thickens. Remove from heat; whisk in egg yolk and extract. Carefully cover surface of caramel with plastic wrap, refrigerate 3 hours or overnight.

prep + cook time 25 minutes (+ refrigeration) **makes** 9
notes You will need 3 x 4 ounce packets round shortbread cookies for this recipe. The cookies should be 2¼ inches in diameter.
Store filled and chocolate-dipped cookies in an airtight container in the fridge for up to a week.

LIME & GINGER KISSES

4 ounces butter, softened
½ cup firmly packed light brown
   sugar
1 egg
¼ cup plain (all-purpose) flour
¼ cup self-raising flour
¾ cup cornstarch
2 teaspoons ground ginger
½ teaspoon ground cinnamon
¼ teaspoon ground cloves
lime butter cream
2 ounces butter, softened
2 teaspoons finely grated
   lime rind
¾ cup confectioners' sugar
2 teaspoons milk

1 Preheat oven to 350°F. Line oven trays with parchment paper.
2 Beat butter, sugar and egg in small bowl with electric mixer until smooth. Stir in sifted dry ingredients.
3 Roll heaped teaspoons of mixture into balls; place balls about 2 inches apart on trays. Bake about 10 minutes. Loosen cookies; cool on trays.
4 Make lime butter cream. Sandwich cookies with butter cream.

lime butter cream Beat butter and rind in small bowl with electric mixer until as white as possible. Beat in sifted confectioners' sugar and milk, in two batches.

prep + cook time 35 minutes (+ cooling) **makes** 18
notes Unfilled cookies will keep in an airtight container for up to a week. Filled cookies will keep for a few days in an airtight container in the fridge.

SPICY FRUIT MINCE PILLOWS

3 ounces butter, softened
⅓ cup confectioners' sugar
1 egg
1¼ cups plain (all-purpose) flour
¼ cup self-raising flour
2 tablespoons milk
2 teaspoons superfine sugar
spicy fruit filling
2⅔ cups seeded dried dates, chopped coarsely
¾ cup water
2 teaspoons ground allspice
¼ teaspoon ground cloves
pinch baking soda

1 Beat butter and sifted confectioners' sugar in small bowl with electric mixer until smooth. Beat in egg until combined. Stir in sifted flours, in two batches. Cover dough; refrigerate 30 minutes.
2 Meanwhile, make spicy fruit filling.
3 Preheat oven to 350°F. Line oven trays with parchment paper.
4 Roll dough between sheets of parchment paper to 12-inch x 16-inch rectangle; cut into four 3-inch x 16-inch strips. Spoon filling into piping bag fitted with large ¾-inch plain tube; pipe filling down center of each strip. Fold edges in until they meet to enclose filling; turn seam-side down onto board. Cut each roll into 10 pillow shapes; place pillows, seam-side down, on trays; brush with milk, sprinkle with superfine sugar.
5 Bake pillows about 20 minutes; cool on trays.

spicy fruit filling Cook dates and the water in medium saucepan, stirring, 10 minutes or until thick and smooth. Stir in spices and baking soda. Cool.

prep + cook time 50 minutes (+ refrigeration) **makes** 40 **note** Pillows will keep in an airtight container at room temperature for up to a week.

HAZELNUT MOMENTS WITH CHOC BERRY FILLING

3 ounces butter, softened
½ teaspoon vanilla extract
¼ cup superfine sugar
1 egg
½ cup ground hazelnuts
¾ cup plain (all-purpose) flour
¼ cup cocoa powder
choc berry filling
3 ounces semi-sweet chocolate, melted
2 ounces butter, softened
⅓ cup chocolate-hazelnut spread
¼ cup fresh raspberries, chopped coarsely

1 Beat butter, extract, sugar and egg in small bowl with electric mixer until combined. Stir in ground hazelnuts, then sifted flour and cocoa.
2 Divide dough in half; roll each half between sheets of parchment paper until ⅛-inch thick. Refrigerate 30 minutes.
3 Preheat oven to 350°F. Line oven trays with parchment paper.
4 Cut dough into 1½-inch fluted rounds; place on trays 1 inch apart. Bake about 8 minutes. Cool on trays.
5 Make choc berry filling.
6 Spoon choc berry filling into piping bag fitted with ¾-inch fluted tube. Pipe filling onto flat side of half the cookies; top with remaining cookies.

choc berry filling Beat cooled chocolate, butter and spread in small bowl with electric mixer until thick and glossy. Fold in raspberries.

prep + cook time 30 minutes (+ refrigeration & cooling)
makes 24
note Unfilled cookies will keep in an airtight container for up to a week. Filled cookies will keep for a few days in an airtight container in the fridge.

COCONUT CHOCOLATE CRUNCHIES

4 ounces butter, softened
¾ cup firmly packed light brown
    sugar
1 tablespoon golden syrup
    or treacle
2 eggs
2 cups self-raising flour
1 cup desiccated coconut
½ cup quick-cooking oats
milk chocolate ganache
6 ounces milk chocolate,
    chopped coarsely
1 ounce butter

1 Preheat oven to 350°F. Line oven trays with parchment paper.
2 Beat butter, sugar and syrup in small bowl with electric mixer until smooth. Beat in eggs, one at a time. Stir in sifted flour, coconut and oats.
3 Roll rounded teaspoons of mixture into balls; place about 2 inches apart on trays. Flatten with fork.
4 Bake cookies about 12 minutes; cool on trays.
5 Meanwhile, make milk chocolate ganache.
6 Sandwich cookies with milk chocolate ganache; refrigerate until firm.

milk chocolate ganache Stir chocolate and butter in small heatproof bowl over small saucepan of simmering water until smooth; cool.

prep + cook time 40 minutes (+ refrigeration & cooling)
makes 40
notes Unfilled cookies will keep in an airtight container for up to a week. Filled cookies will keep for a few days in an airtight container in the fridge.

WAGONETTES

⅓ cup superfine sugar
⅓ cup water
2 teaspoons gelatin
⅓ cup strawberry jam (conserve), warmed, strained
32 milk-chocolate wheat biscuits (see notes)
½ teaspoon vanilla extract
pink food coloring

1 Combine sugar and half the water in small saucepan; stir over low heat until sugar dissolves.
2 Combine gelatin and the remaining water in small jug. Pour gelatin mixture into hot sugar syrup; stir over medium heat about 3 minutes or until gelatine dissolves. Pour mixture into small heatproof bowl; cool.
3 Spread jam onto the plain side of half the cookies.
4 To make marshmallow, beat gelatin mixture in small bowl with electric mixer on high speed for about 8 minutes or until very thick. Beat in extract and a few drops of coloring.
5 Spoon marshmallow into piping bag fitted with ¾-inch plain tube. Pipe marshmallow over jam; top with remaining cookies.

prep + cook time 30 minutes (+ cooling) **makes** 16
notes You need 2 x 6½- ounce packets milk chocolate wheat cookies for this recipe.
If the marshmallow sets too quickly, return it to the mixer bowl with about 1 tablespoon boiling water and beat it for about a minute. Unfilled cookies will keep in an airtight container for up to a week. Filled cookies will keep for a few days in an airtight container in the fridge.

GOLDEN OATY CARROT COOKIES

4 ounces butter, softened
1 cup firmly packed light brown
   sugar
1 egg yolk
½ cup firmly packed coarsely
   grated carrot
1½ cups plain (all-purpose) flour
½ teaspoon baking soda
1 teaspoon ground cinnamon
1 cup rolled oats
1 tablespoon milk,
   approximately

1 Preheat oven to 350°F. Line
oven trays with parchment paper.
2 Beat butter, sugar and egg
yolk in small bowl with electric
mixer until combined. Stir in
carrot, then sifted flour, soda and
cinnamon. Stir in oats and enough
milk to make a firm dough.
3 Roll heaped teaspoons of
mixture into balls. Place balls
about 2 inches apart on trays;
flatten slightly.
4 Bake cookies about 15 minutes;
cool on trays.

prep + cook time 35 minutes
makes 44
note Store cookies in an airtight
container for up to a week.

PASSIONFRUIT MERINGUE KISSES

2 egg whites
½ cup superfine sugar
yellow food coloring
1 teaspoon strained
    passionfruit juice
1 teaspoon cornstarch
passionfruit butter
2 ounces unsalted butter,
    softened
¾ cup confectioners' sugar
1 tablespoon passionfruit pulp

1 Preheat oven to 250°F.
Grease oven trays; line with
parchment paper.
2 Beat egg whites, superfine
sugar and a few drops of
coloring in small bowl with
electric mixer about 15 minutes
or until sugar is dissolved. Fold
in juice and cornflour.
3 Spoon mixture into piping bag
fitted with ¾-inch fluted tube;
pipe 1½-inch stars onto trays ¾
inch apart.
4 Bake meringues about 1 hour.
Cool on trays.
5 Meanwhile, make passionfruit
butter.
6 Sandwich meringues with
passionfruit butter.
passionfruit butter Beat butter
and sifted confectioners' sugar
in small bowl with electric mixer
until light and fluffy. Stir in pulp.

prep + cook time
1 hour 25 minutes (+ cooling)
makes 24

MINT SLICE COOKIES

2 ounces butter, softened
¼ cup superfine sugar
1 egg
½ teaspoon vanilla extract
1 cup plain (all-purpose) flour
2 tablespoons cocoa powder
2 teaspoons milk, approximately
48 soft chocolate-coated mints
6 ounces semi-sweet chocolate,
  melted

1 Beat butter, sugar, egg and extract in small bowl with electric mixer until combined. Stir in sifted flour and cocoa and enough milk to make a firm dough. Cover dough; refrigerate 30 minutes.
2 Preheat oven to 350°F. Line oven trays with parchment paper.
3 Roll dough between sheets of parchment paper until ¼-inch thick; cut 1¼-inch rounds from dough. Place rounds about 1 inch apart on trays.
4 Bake cookies about 10 minutes; immediately place one chocolate mint on top of each cookie, press down lightly. Cool on trays.
5 Place cookies on wire rack over parchment-paper-lined tray; drizzle with chocolate. Stand at room temperature until set.

prep + cook time 45 minutes (+ refrigeration & standing)
makes 48
notes Unfilled cookies will keep in an airtight container for up to a week. Filled cookies will keep for a few days in an airtight container in the fridge. We used individually wrapped chocolate-coated mints for this recipe. They come in a 5½ ounce box of 24 chocolates.

Biscotti

JAFFA BISCOTTI

1 cup superfine sugar
2 eggs
1⅓ cups plain (all-purpose) flour
⅓ cup self-raising flour
¼ cup cocoa powder
¾ cup finely chopped glacé
   orange

1 Preheat oven to 350°F. Grease oven tray.
2 Whisk sugar and eggs in medium bowl until combined; stir in sifted flours and cocoa, then orange.
3 Knead dough on floured surface until smooth. Divide dough in half, roll each portion into a 12-inch log; place logs on tray.
4 Bake logs about 30 minutes. Cool on tray 10 minutes.
5 Reduce oven to 300°F.
6 Using serrated knife, cut logs diagonally into ¼-inch slices. Arrange slices, in single layer, on ungreased oven trays. Bake about 30 minutes or until biscotti are dry and crisp, turning halfway through baking. Cool on wire racks.

prep + cook time
1 hour 25 minutes **makes** 60
notes You will need about 8 slices glacé orange for this recipe. Biscotti will keep in an airtight container for at least a month.

CITRUS COCONUT BISCOTTI

1 cup superfine sugar
2 eggs
1⅓ cups plain (all-purpose) flour
⅓ cup self-raising flour
1 cup desiccated coconut
2 teaspoons each finely
   grated lemon, lime and
   orange rinds

1 Preheat oven to 350°F.
Grease oven tray.
2 Whisk sugar and eggs in
medium bowl until combined;
stir in sifted flours then coconut
and rinds.
3 Knead dough on floured
surface until smooth. Divide
dough in half, roll each portion
into a 12-inch log; place logs
on tray.
4 Bake logs about 30 minutes.
Cool on tray 10 minutes.
5 Reduce oven to 300°F.
6 Using serrated knife, cut logs
diagonally into ¼-inch slices.
Arrange slices, in single layer,
on ungreased oven trays. Bake
about 30 minutes or until biscotti
are dry and crisp, turning halfway
through baking. Cool on wire
racks.

prep + cook time
1 hour 25 minutes **makes** 60
note Biscotti will keep in an
airtight container for at least
a month.

ROSY APRICOT & PISTACHIO BISCOTTI

1 cup superfine sugar
2 eggs
1⅓ cups plain (all-purpose) flour
⅓ cup self-raising flour
⅓ cup finely chopped dried
    apricots
⅓ cup unsalted roasted
    pistachios
4 teaspoons rosewater

1 Preheat oven to 350°F. Grease oven tray.
2 Whisk sugar and eggs in medium bowl until combined; stir in sifted flours then apricots, nuts and rosewater.
3 Knead dough on floured surface until smooth. Divide dough in half, roll each portion into a 8-inch log; place logs on tray.
4 Bake logs about 30 minutes. Cool on tray 10 minutes.
5 Reduce oven to 300°F.
6 Using serrated knife, cut logs diagonally into ¼-inch slices. Arrange slices, in single layer, on ungreased oven trays. Bake about 30 minutes or until biscotti are dry and crisp, turning halfway through baking. Cool on wire racks.

prep + cook time
1 hour 25 minutes **makes** 40
note Biscotti will keep in an airtight container for at least a month.

APPLE, CRANBERRY &
WHITE CHOCOLATE BISCOTTI

1 cup superfine sugar
2 eggs
1⅓ cups plain (all-purpose) flour
⅓ cup self-raising flour
½ cup finely chopped dried
   apple
½ cup coarsely chopped dried
   cranberries
3 ounces white chocolate,
   grated coarsely

1 Preheat oven to 350°F. Grease oven tray.
2 Whisk sugar and eggs in medium bowl until combined; stir in sifted flours then apple, cranberries and chocolate.
3 Knead dough on floured surface until smooth. Divide dough in half, roll each portion into a 12-inch log; place logs on tray.
4 Bake logs about 30 minutes. Cool on tray 10 minutes.
5 Reduce oven to 300°F.
6 Using serrated knife, cut logs diagonally into ¼-inch slices. Arrange slices, in single layer, on ungreased oven trays. Bake about 30 minutes or until biscotti are dry and crisp, turning halfway through baking. Cool on wire racks.

prep + cook time
1 hour 25 minutes **makes** 60
note Biscotti will keep in an airtight container for at least a month.

TRIPLE CHOCOLATE BISCOTTI WITH HAZELNUTS

1 ounce butter, softened
½ cup firmly packed light brown sugar
1 teaspoon vanilla extract
3 eggs
¾ cup plain (all-purpose) flour
¼ cup self-raising flour
⅓ cup cocoa powder
1 cup roasted hazelnuts, chopped coarsely
2 ounces semi-sweet chocolate, chopped finely
1 ounce milk chocolate, chopped finely
2 ounces white chocolate, chopped finely

1 Beat butter, sugar and extract in small bowl with electric mixer until combined. Add eggs, beat until combined (mixture will curdle at this stage, but will come together later). Stir in sifted dry ingredients, then nuts and chocolates. Cover mixture, refrigerate 1 hour.

2 Preheat oven to 350°F. Grease oven trays.

3 Divide dough in half, roll each portion into a 6-inch log; place logs on tray.

4 Bake logs about 25 minutes. Cool on trays.

5 Reduce oven to 300°F.

6 Using serrated knife, cut logs diagonally into ½-inch slices. Arrange slices, in single layer, on ungreased oven trays. Bake about 30 minutes or until biscotti are dry and crisp, turning halfway through baking. Cool on wire racks.

prep + cook time
1 hour 10 minutes (+ refrigeration)
makes 30
note Biscotti will keep in an airtight container for at least a month.

ALMOND BREAD

3 egg whites
½ cup superfine sugar
1 cup plain (all-purpose) flour
¾ cup almond slivers

1 Preheat oven to 350°F. Grease 4-inch x 8-inch loaf pan.
2 Beat egg whites in small bowl with electric mixer until soft peaks form. Gradually add sugar, beating until dissolved between additions. Fold in sifted flour and nuts; spread mixture into pan.
3 Bake almond bread about 30 minutes. Cool bread in pan. Remove bread from pan, wrap in foil; stand overnight.
4 Preheat oven to 300°F.
5 Using a sharp serrated knife, cut the bread into wafer-thin slices. Arrange slices, in single layer, on ungreased oven trays. Bake about 45 minutes or until dry and crisp.

prep + cook time
1 hour 35 minutes (+ cooling & standing) **makes** 40
note Almond bread will keep in an airtight container for months.

COFFEE & WALNUT BISCOTTI

½ cup superfine sugar
1 egg
½ cup plain (all-purpose) flour
¼ cup self-raising flour
4 teaspoons instant coffee
  granules
1 cup walnuts, chopped coarsely
3 ounces semi-sweet chocolate,
  melted

1 Preheat oven to 350°F. Grease oven tray.
2 Whisk sugar and egg in medium bowl until combined; stir in sifted flours, then coffee granules and walnuts.
3 Shape dough into an 8-inch log; place on tray.
4 Bake log about 30 minutes. Cool on tray.
5 Reduce oven to 300°F.
6 Using serrated knife, cut log diagonally into ½-inch slices. Arrange slices, in single layer, on ungreased oven trays. Bake about 30 minutes or until biscotti are dry and crisp, turning halfway through baking. Cool on wire racks.
7 Spread chocolate over one side of each biscotti; stand at room temperature until set.

prep + cook time
1 hour 10 minutes (+ standing)
makes 20
note Biscotti will keep in an airtight container for at least a month.

GINGERBREAD BISCOTTI

½ cup firmly packed dark brown
  sugar
1 egg
½ cup plain (all-purpose) flour
¼ cup self-raising flour
4 teaspoons ground ginger
1 teaspoon ground cinnamon
¼ teaspoon ground cloves
½ cup coarsely chopped glacé
  ginger
lemon glacé icing
1 cup confectioners' sugar
½ teaspoon finely grated
  lemon rind
¼ cup lemon juice

1 Preheat oven to 350°F.
Grease oven tray.
2 Whisk sugar and egg in
medium bowl until combined;
stir in sifted dry ingredients,
then glacé ginger.
3 Shape dough into an 8-inch
log; place on tray.
4 Bake log about 30 minutes.
Cool on tray.
5 Reduce oven to 300°F.
6 Using serrated knife, cut log
diagonally into ¼-inch slices.
Arrange slices, in single layer,
on ungreased oven trays. Bake
about 30 minutes or until biscotti
are dry and crisp, turning halfway
through baking. Cool on wire
racks.
7 Meanwhile, make lemon
glacé icing.
8 Dip one end of each biscotti
into icing, place on foil-lined tray;
stand at room temperature
until set.

lemon glacé icing Stir sifted
confectioners' sugar, rind and
juice in small bowl until smooth.

prep + cook time
1 hour 10 minutes (+ standing)
makes 40
note Biscotti will keep in an
airtight container for at least
a month.

Bars

TURKISH DELIGHT BARS

6 ounces unsalted butter, softened

⅓ cup superfine sugar

1 teaspoon vanilla extract

1½ cups plain (all-purpose) flour

⅓ cup self-raising flour

4 teaspoons gelatin

2 tablespoons water

⅓ cup water, extra

1½ cups white (granulated) sugar

⅓ cup cornstarch

2 tablespoons rosewater

red food coloring

2 tablespoons confectioners' sugar

1 Preheat oven to 350°F. Grease 8-inch x 12-inch rectangular pan; line base and long sides with parchment paper, extending paper 2 inches over sides.

2 Beat butter, superfine sugar and extract in small bowl with electric mixer until combined. Stir in sifted flours. Press mixture evenly over base of pan; using fork, rough the surface. Bake base about 20 minutes or until golden brown. Cool.

3 Sprinkle gelatin over the water in small heatproof container; stand container in small saucepan of simmering water, stir until gelatin dissolves.

4 Reserve 1 tablespoon of the extra water. Stir the remaining extra water and white sugar in medium saucepan over low heat, without boiling, until sugar dissolves; bring to the boil. Boil, uncovered, without stirring, until temperature reaches 240°F on a candy thermometer. Reduce heat; simmer, uncovered, 5 minutes, without stirring, regulating heat to maintain temperature at 240°F. Remove from heat.

5 Blend cornstarch with the reserved 1 tablespoon water, gelatine mixture, rosewater and a few drops of food coloring until smooth; stir into sugar syrup. Return to heat; simmer, stirring, about 3 minutes or until mixture is opaque. Strain mixture over bar base, skim any scum from surface; stand 3 hours or overnight at room temperature.

6 Sprinkle with sifted confectioners' sugar to serve.

prep + cook time 1 hour (+ standing) **makes** 24

notes It's important to use a candy thermometer for guaranteed success with this recipe. Bars can be stored, refrigerated in an airtight container, for up to four days. Use a hot wet knife to cut the bar.

FRUITY CHOC CHIP BARS

⅓ cup firmly packed light brown
   sugar
3 ounces butter, chopped
   coarsely
1¼ cups plain (all-purpose) flour
1 egg yolk
fruity choc topping
2 eggs
1 cup firmly packed light brown
   sugar
⅓ cup self-raising flour
1 cup milk choc chips
1 cup rolled oats
½ cup shredded coconut
⅓ cup coarsely chopped,
   unsalted, roasted pistachios
½ cup finely chopped dried
   mixed berries
½ cup finely chopped dried
   apple

1 Preheat oven to 350°F. Grease 8-inch x 12-inch rectangular pan; line base and long sides with parchment paper, extending paper 2 inches over sides.
2 Stir sugar and butter in medium saucepan over low heat until smooth. Remove from heat; stir in sifted flour, then egg yolk. Press mixture firmly over base of pan; bake about 10 minutes or until browned lightly. Cool.
3 Meanwhile, make fruity choc topping.
4 Spread topping over base; bake about 25 minutes or until browned lightly. Cool in pan.

fruity choc topping Beat eggs and sugar in small bowl with electric mixer until thick and pale, transfer to large bowl; fold in sifted flour, then remaining ingredients.

prep + cook time 1 hour
makes 24
note Bars can be stored in an airtight container for up to a week.

HEDGEHOG BARS

14 ounces canned sweetened
  condensed milk
3 ounces unsalted butter,
  chopped coarsely
6 ounces semi-sweet chocolate,
  chopped coarsely
8 ounces plain sweet cookies
⅔ cup roasted hazelnuts
⅔ cup raisins

1 Grease 8-inch x 12-inch rectangular pan; line base and long sides with baking paper, extending paper 2 inches over sides.
2 Stir condensed milk and butter in medium saucepan over medium heat until smooth. Remove from heat; add chocolate, stir until smooth.
3 Break cookies into small pieces; place in large bowl with nuts and raisins. Stir in chocolate mixture.
4 Press mixture firmly into pan. Refrigerate 2 hours or until firm.

prep + cook time 20 minutes (+ refrigeration) **makes** 20
note We used plain sweet shortbread cookies.

WHITE CHOCOLATE &
BERRY CHEESECAKE BARS

8 ounces ginger snap cookies
2 teaspoons gelatin
¼ cup boiling water
12 ounces softened cream
  cheese
⅓ cup superfine sugar
1¼ cups cream
6 ounces white chocolate,
  melted
4 ounces frozen mixed berries
3 ounces frozen mixed berries,
  extra

1 Grease deep 8-inch square
cake pan.
2 Place cookies in base of pan.
3 Sprinkle gelatin over water in
small heatproof container; stand
container in small saucepan of
simmering water, stir until gelatin
dissolves. Cool 5 minutes.
4 Meanwhile, beat cream
cheese and sugar in small bowl
with electric mixer until smooth;
beat in cream. Stir in gelatin
mixture, chocolate and berries.
Pour filling into pan; sprinkle with
extra berries.
5 Refrigerate cheesecake 3 hours
or overnight.

prep time 30 minutes
(+ refrigeration) **makes** 20
note It is fine to use just 10 oz.
of cream in this recipe.

RICH CHOCOLATE HAZELNUT BARS

8 ounces plain chocolate
cookies
¾ cup roasted hazelnuts,
coarsely chopped
5 ounces unsalted butter, melted
14 ounces canned sweetened
condensed milk
12 ounces milk chocolate,
chopped coarsely
10 ounces semi-sweet chocolate,
chopped coarsely
½ ounce unsalted butter, extra
1 ounce white chocolate, melted

1 Grease 8-inch x 12-inch rectangular pan; line base and long sides with parchment paper, extending paper 2 inches over sides.
2 Process cookies and ¼ cup of the nuts until fine; add butter, process until combined. Press mixture over base of pan. Refrigerate about 20 minutes or until firm.
3 Stir condensed milk and 11 ounces of the milk chocolate in small saucepan over low heat until smooth. Stir in remaining nuts. Working quickly, spread chocolate mixture over base.

4 Stir semi-sweet chocolate and extra butter in small saucepan over low heat until smooth. Spread over milk chocolate layer.
5 Melt remaining milk chocolate; drizzle milk and white chocolate over pan. Refrigerate 20 minutes or until firm.

prep + cook time 30 minutes (+ refrigeration) **makes** 32
note Bars will keep in an airtight container in the fridge for up to a week.

PEAR & RASPBERRY STREUSEL BARS

3 medium pears, peeled, cored,
   sliced thinly
¼ cup superfine sugar
¼ cup water
3 ounces butter, softened
⅓ cup superfine sugar, extra
1 egg
1 cup self-raising flour
⅓ cup milk
5 ounces fresh or frozen
   raspberries
¼ cup finely chopped walnuts
streusel topping
⅓ cup plain (all-purpose) flour
2 tablespoons self-raising flour
¼ cup firmly packed light brown
   sugar
1 teaspoon mixed spice
3 ounces cold butter, chopped
   coarsely

1 Make streusel topping.
2 Preheat oven to 350°F. Grease
8-inch x 12-inch rectangular pan;
line base and long sides with
parchment paper, extending
paper 2 inches over sides.
3 Combine pear, sugar and the
water in large saucepan; cook,
covered, stirring occasionally,
about 10 minutes or until pear
softens. Drain, then cool.
4 Beat butter and extra sugar
in small bowl with electric mixer
until light and fluffy. Add egg;
beat until combined. Stir in sifted
flour and milk, in two batches.
Spread mixture into pan.
5 Bake base 15 minutes.
Remove from oven.
6 Increase oven to 400°F.
7 Working quickly, arrange
pear over base; sprinkle with
raspberries and nuts. Coarsely
grate streusel over fruit mixture.
8 Bake about 20 minutes.
Stand in pan 10 minutes
before turning, top-side-up,
onto wire rack to cool. Serve
warm or cold.

streusel topping Process
ingredients until combined.
Wrap in plastic; freeze 1 hour or
until firm.

prep + cook time
1 hour 10 minutes (+ freezing &
cooling) **makes** 12
notes This recipe is best served
warm and would be delicious as
a dessert with ice-cream. Bars
will keep in an airtight container
in the fridge for two days.

CHOCOLATE CARAMEL BARS

½ cup self-raising flour
½ cup plain (all-purpose) flour
1 cup desiccated coconut
1 cup firmly packed light brown
  sugar
4 ounces butter, melted
14 ounces canned sweetened
  condensed milk
1 ounce butter, extra
2 tablespoons golden syrup
  or treacle
6 ounces semi-sweet chocolate,
  chopped coarsely
2 teaspoons vegetable oil

1 Preheat oven to 350°F. Grease
8-inch x 12-inch rectangular pan;
line base and long sides with
parchment paper, extending
paper 2 inches over sides.
2 Combine sifted flours, coconut,
sugar and butter in medium
bowl; press mixture evenly over
base of pan.
3 Bake base about 15 minutes
or until browned lightly.
4 Meanwhile, stir condensed
milk, extra butter and syrup in
small saucepan over medium
heat about 15 minutes or until
caramel mixture is golden brown;
pour over base.
5 Bake 10 minutes; cool.
6 Stir chocolate and oil in small
saucepan over low heat until
smooth. Pour warm topping over
cold caramel. Refrigerate 3 hours
or overnight.

prep + cook time 45 minutes
(+ cooling & refrigeration)
makes 24
note The bars will keep in an
airtight container in the fridge
for up to four days.

BLUEBERRY MACARON BARS

3 ounces butter, melted
½ cup superfine sugar
1 egg
⅔ cup plain (all-purpose) flour
¼ cup self-raising flour
1 tablespoon vanilla instant
    pudding mix
½ cup blueberry jam (conserve)
coconut topping
2 egg whites, beaten lightly
2½ cups shredded coconut
¼ cup superfine sugar

1 Preheat oven to 350°F. Grease 8-inch x 12-inch rectangular pan; line base and long sides with parchment paper, extending paper 2 inches over sides.
2 Beat butter, sugar and egg in small bowl with electric mixer until combined; stir in sifted flours and custard powder. Spread dough into pan; spread with jam.
3 Make coconut topping; sprinkle over jam.
4 Bake about 40 minutes; cool in pan.

coconut topping Combine ingredients in medium bowl.

prep + cook time 1 hour
makes 32
note Bars can be stored in an airtight container for up to a week.

CHOC-CARAMEL BARS

2 x 6½-ounce chocolate filled chocolate-coated cookies
1½ ounces unsalted butter, chopped
⅓ cup sweetened condensed milk
6 ounces caramels, chopped coarsely

chocolate topping
8 ounces milk chocolate, chopped coarsely
2 teaspoons vegetable oil

1 Grease 8-inch x 12-inch rectangular pan; line base and long sides with parchment paper, extending paper 2 inches over sides.
2 Process half the cookies until fine. Chop remaining cookies coarsely.
3 Stir butter and condensed milk in small saucepan over low heat until smooth.
4 Combine processed and chopped cookies with caramels in medium bowl; stir in butter mixture. Press mixture firmly into pan. Refrigerate 30 minutes.
5 Meanwhile, make chocolate topping.
6 Spread chocolate topping over slice. Refrigerate about 30 minutes or until firm.

chocolate topping Stir ingredients in small heatproof bowl over small saucepan of simmering water until smooth.

prep + cook time 30 minutes (+ refrigeration) makes 20
notes The bars will keep in an airtight container in the fridge for up to four days.

CHOCOLATE BROWNIE BARS

4 ounces butter, chopped
6 ounces semi-sweet chocolate, chopped coarsely
½ cup superfine sugar
2 eggs
1¼ cups plain (all-purpose) flour
5 ounces white chocolate, chopped
3 ounces milk chocolate, chopped

1 Preheat oven to 350°F. Grease deep 8-inch square cake pan; line base with parchment paper, extending paper 2 inches over sides.
2 Stir butter and dark chocolate in medium saucepan over low heat until smooth. Cool 10 minutes.
3 Stir in sugar and eggs, then sifted flour, white chocolate and milk chocolate. Spread mixture into pan.
4 Bake about 35 minutes. Cool in pan.

prep + cook time 1 hour
makes 25

HONEY & COCONUT MUESLI BARS

2½ cups rolled oats
1 cup puffed rice cereal
½ cup shredded coconut
½ cup slivered almonds
1 tablespoon honey
14 ounces canned sweetened
    condensed milk

1 Preheat oven to 325°F. Grease
9-inch x 13-inch swiss roll pan;
line base and long sides with
parchment, extending paper
2 inches over sides.
2 Combine ingredients in
large bowl; press mixture firmly
into pan.
3 Bake about 40 minutes or
until browned lightly. Cool in pan.

prep + cook time 50 minutes
makes 36

LATTICE BARS WITH PASSIONFRUIT ICING

2 teaspoons gelatin
2 tablespoons water
8 ounces cream cheese,
  softened
8 ounces unsalted butter,
  softened
½ cup superfine sugar
1 teaspoon vanilla extract
2 tablespoons lemon juice
35 square lattice cookies
  (see notes)

passionfruit icing
2 cups confectioners' sugar
2 teaspoons unsalted butter
2 tablespoons passionfruit pulp
2 teaspoons hot water,
  approximately

1 Grease 8-inch x 12-inch rectangular pan; line base and long sides with parchment paper, extending paper 2 inches over sides.
2 Sprinkle gelatin over the water in small heatproof jug; stand jug in small saucepan of simmering water, stir until gelatin dissolves.
3 Beat cream cheese, butter, sugar and extract in small bowl with electric mixer until smooth. Stir in juice and gelatin mixture.
4 Line base of pan with half the cookies; trim cookies to fit, if necessary. Spread cream cheese filling evenly over cookies base; top with remaining cookies.
5 Make passionfruit icing.
6 Spread icing over cookies. Refrigerate 3 hours or overnight.

passionfruit icing Sift confectioners' sugar into small heatproof bowl; stir in butter, passionfruit and enough of the water to make a thick paste. Place bowl over small saucepan of simmering water; stir until icing is spreadable.

prep + cook time 30 minutes (+ refrigeration) **makes** 12
notes You need to buy 2 packets of lattice cookies for this recipe. The bar will keep in an airtight container in the fridge for up to four days.

APPLE STREUSEL BARS

7 ounces unsalted butter, softened
1 cup superfine sugar
2 egg yolks
1⅓ cups plain (all-purpose) flour
½ cup self-raising flour
2 tablespoons vanilla instant pudding
4 large apples, sliced thinly
1 tablespoon honey
1 teaspoon finely grated lemon rind

streusel topping
½ cup plain (all-purpose) flour
¼ cup self-raising flour
⅓ cup firmly packed light brown sugar
½ teaspoon ground cinnamon
3 ounces unsalted butter, chopped coarsely

1 Make streusel topping.
2 Preheat oven to 350°F. Grease 8-inch x 12-inch rectangular pan; line base and long sides with parchment paper, extending paper 2 inches over sides.
3 Beat butter, sugar and egg yolks in small bowl with electric mixer until light and fluffy, transfer to large bowl; stir in sifted flours and vanilla instant pudding. Press mixture into pan.
4 Bake base 25 minutes. Cool 15 minutes.
5 Meanwhile, cook apple, honey and rind, covered, in medium saucepan, stirring occasionally, about 5 minutes or until apples are tender. Remove from heat; drain, cool 15 minutes.
6 Spread apple mixture over base; coarsely grate streusel topping over apple.
7 Bake bar about 20 minutes. Cool bar in pan.

streusel topping Process ingredients until combined. Enclose in plastic wrap; freeze 1 hour or until firm.

prep + cook time 1 hour (+ freezing & cooling)
makes 12
note Will keep in an airtight container in the fridge for up to three days.

BAKEWELL BARS

5 ounces unsalted butter,
  softened
¼ cup superfine sugar
2 egg yolks
1½ cups plain (all-purpose) flour
¾ cup ground almonds
¾ cup strawberry jam (conserve)
almond filling
6 ounces unsalted butter,
  softened
1 teaspoon finely grated
  lemon rind
¾ cup superfine sugar
3 eggs
1¼ cups ground almonds
¼ cup plain (all-purpose) flour
lemon icing
2 cups confectioners' sugar
¼ cup lemon juice,
  approximately

1 Beat butter, sugar and egg yolks in small bowl with electric mixer until combined. Stir in sifted flour and ground almonds, in two batches. Knead pastry gently on floured surface until smooth. Enclose in plastic wrap; refrigerate 30 minutes.
2 Make almond filling.
3 Meanwhile, preheat oven to 400°F.
4 Grease 8-inch x 12-inch rectangular pan; line base and long sides with parchment paper, extending paper 2 inches over sides.
5 Roll out pastry between sheets of parchment paper until large enough to line pan; press into base and sides, trim edge. Spread jam then almond filling evenly over base.
6 Bake about 30 minutes. Cool in pan.
7 Make lemon icing.
8 Spread icing over bars; stand at room temperature until icing is set.

almond filling Beat butter, rind and sugar in small bowl with electric mixer until light and fluffy. Beat in eggs, one at a time. Stir in ground almonds and sifted flour.
lemon icing Sift confectioners' sugar into small bowl; stir in enough of the juice until icing is spreadable.

prep + cook time
1 hour 10 minutes (+ refrigeration & standing) **makes** 32
note Can be stored in an airtight container for up to a week.

FRUIT MINCE BARS

1½ cups plain (all-purpose) flour
1¼ cups self-raising flour
5 ounces cold butter, chopped
1 tablespoon golden syrup
   or treacle
1 egg
⅓ cup milk, approximately
2 teaspoons milk, extra
1 tablespoon turbinado sugar
fruit mince
16 ounces mixed dried fruit,
   chopped coarsely
½ cup water
½ cup firmly packed dark brown
   sugar
1 tablespoon orange marmalade
2 teaspoons finely grated
   orange rind
2 tablespoons orange juice

1 Make fruit mince.
2 Grease 8-inch x 12-inch rectangular pan; line base and long sides with parchment paper, extending paper 2 inches over sides.
3 Sift flours into large bowl; rub in butter until mixture is crumbly. Stir in combined syrup and egg and enough milk to make a firm dough. Knead dough gently on floured surface until smooth. Refrigerate 30 minutes.
4 Preheat oven to 400°F.
5 Divide dough in half. Roll one half between sheets of parchment paper until large enough to cover base of pan; press into pan, spread fruit mince over dough.
6 Roll remaining dough between sheets of parchment paper until large enough to cover fruit mince; place on top of fruit mince, trim to fit. Brush with extra milk; sprinkle with turbinado sugar.
7 Bake about 20 minutes. Cool in pan before cutting.

fruit mince Cook ingredients in medium saucepan, stirring, over medium heat, about 10 minutes or until thick. Cool.

prep + cook time 50 minutes (+ refrigeration & cooling)
makes 24
notes Use white (granulated) sugar instead of the turbinado, if you like. Can be stored in an airtight container for up to a week.

LIME & COCONUT BARS

7½ ounces plain sweet cookies
½ cup sweetened condensed
   milk
3 ounces unsalted butter,
   chopped
1 teaspoon finely grated
   lime rind
1 tablespoon lime juice
½ cup shredded coconut
lime icing
2 cups confectioners' sugar
½ ounce unsalted butter, melted
2 tablespoons lime juice

1 Grease 8-inch x 12-inch rectangular pan; line base and long sides with parchment paper, extending paper 2 inches over sides.
2 Process 6 ounces of the cookies until fine; chop remaining cookies coarsely.
3 Stir condensed milk and butter in small saucepan over medium heat until smooth.
4 Combine processed and chopped cookies, rind, juice and coconut in medium bowl. Add condensed milk mixture; stir to combine. Press mixture firmly into pan. Refrigerate 30 minutes or until firm.
5 Meanwhile, make lime icing.
6 Spread icing over bars. Refrigerate 30 minutes or until firm.

lime icing Sift confectioners' sugar into small heatproof bowl; stir in butter, juice and enough water to make a thick paste. Place bowl over small saucepan of simmering water, stir until icing is spreadable.

prep + cook time 25 minutes (+ refrigeration) **makes** 24

DOUBLE-CHOCOLATE BARS

4 ounces butter, chopped
   coarsely
1 cup firmly packed dark brown
   sugar
6 ounces semi-sweet chocolate
1¼ cups rolled oats
¾ cup coarsely chopped walnuts
1 egg
¾ cup plain (all-purpose) flour
¼ cup self-raising flour
½ teaspoon baking soda
⅔ cup dark choc chips

1 Preheat oven to 325°F. Grease 8-inch x 12-inch rectangular pan; line base and long sides with parchment paper, extending paper 2 inches over sides.
2 Melt butter in medium saucepan over low heat. Remove from heat; stir in sugar until smooth.
3 Coarsely chop half the semi-sweet chocolate.
4 Stir oats and nuts into butter mixture, then egg, sifted dry ingredients, chopped chocolate and choc chips. Spread mixture evenly into pan.
5 Bake about 30 minutes. Cover with foil; cool.
6 Melt remaining semi-sweet chocolate. Turn top-side-up, onto wire rack; drizzle with melted chocolate. Stand at room temperature until set before cutting.

prep + cook time 45 minutes (+ cooling & standing)
makes 30
note Can be stored in an airtight container for up to a week.

GLOSSARY

allspice also called pimento or jamaican pepper; it tastes like a combination of cumin, nutmeg, clove and cinnamon. It is available whole (pea-sized berry) or ground.

almonds
blanched whole nuts with brown skins removed.
essence also known as extract.
ground also known as almond meal; nuts are powdered to a coarse flour-like texture.

baking soda a raising agent used in baking.

cookie
chocolate wheat cookie wheatmeal-based cookie, topped with milk or dark chocolate.
lattice an open-weave square-shaped cookie. These flaky pastry cookies are made from flour, oil, sugar and milk powder. The dough is gently rolled into very fine sheets, just like flaky pastry, and is then glazed with a light sprinkling of sugar before being baked until puffed and golden.
plain chocolate a crisp sweet cookie with added cocoa powder but having no icing or filling.
plain sweet a crisp sweet cookie without icing or any fillings.
shortbread a pale golden, crumbly, buttery-tasting cookie made of butter, sugar and flour (generally one part sugar, two parts butter and three parts flour).
Tim Tam chocolate cookies coated in melted chocolate; made from chocolate, flour, sugar, oil, golden syrup, milk powder and cocoa.

butter use salted or unsalted (sweet) butter; 8 tbsp is equal to one stick.

caramel top caramel filling made from milk and cane sugar. Can be used straight from the can for cheesecakes, slices and tarts. Is similar to sweetened condensed milk, only has a thicker, caramel consistency.

chocolate
semi-sweet also known as luxury chocolate; made of a high percentage of cocoa liquor and cocoa butter, and a little added sugar. Unless stated otherwise, we use semi-sweet chocolate in this book.
milk the most popular eating chocolate, mild and very sweet; similar to dark with the difference being the addition of milk solids.
peppermint cream a confectionery with a peppermint fondant centre that is covered in dark chocolate.
peppermint crisp a chocolate bar with a crisp peppermint centre covered with dark chocolate.
white contains no cocoa solids but derives its sweet flavour from cocoa butter. Is very sensitive to heat, so watch carefully when melting.
chocolate-hazelnut spread we use Nutella in this book.

cinnamon dried inner bark of the shoots of the cinnamon tree; available in stick (quill) or ground form.

cloves dried flower buds of a tropical tree; can be used whole or in ground form. Has a distinctively pungent and 'spicy' scent and flavour.

cocoa powder also known as cocoa; dried, unsweetened, roasted then ground cocoa beans (cacao seeds).

corn flakes commercially manufactured cereal made of dehydrated, then baked crisp flakes of corn.

cornstarch used as a thickening agent. Available as 100% corn (maize) and wheaten cornflour.

cream
pouring also called fresh or pure cream. It has no additives and a minimum fat content 35%.
thickened a whipping cream containing a thickener; has a minimum fat content 35%.

cream cheese commonly known as Philadelphia or Philly, a soft cows'-milk cheese with a fat content of at least 33%. Sold at supermarkets in bulk or in smaller-sized packages.

cream of tartar the acid ingredient in baking powder; added to confectionery mixtures to help prevent sugar from crystallizing. Keeps frostings creamy and improves volume when beating egg whites.

flour
plain (all-purpose) made from wheat.
rice a very fine flour made from ground white rice.
self-raising plain flour that has been sifted with baking powder in the proportion of 1 cup flour to 2 teaspoons baking powder.
wholewheat milled from whole wheat grain (bran, germ and endosperm). Available as plain or self-raising.

food coloring dyes that can be used to change the color of various foods. These dyes can be eaten and do not change the taste to a noticeable extent.

fruit, glacé have been preserved by boiling in a heavy sugar syrup.

gelatin if using gelatin leaves, three teaspoons of powdered gelatin (or one sachet) is roughly equivalent to four gelatin leaves.

ginger, ground also called powdered ginger; used as a flavoring in cakes, pies and puddings but cannot be substituted for fresh ginger.

golden syrup a by-product of refined sugarcane; pure maple syrup or honey can be substituted.

hazelnuts, ground hazelnuts ground into a coarse or fine powder. Also known as hazelnut meal.

jam also called preserve or conserve; most often made from fruit.

jersey caramels two layers of sweet condensed milk caramel that sandwiches a layer of white caramel. Soft, chewy and sweet.

liqueurs
coconut-flavored we used Malibu, but you can use your favorite coconut-flavored liqueur.

limoncello a digestive (an alcoholic drink that is used to stimulate or assist digestion; usually taken at the end of the meal). Made from the peel only of fragrant lemons; peel is steeped in good-quality clear alcohol then diluted with sugar and water.

malted milk powder a combination of wheat flour, malt flour and milk, which are evaporated to give the powder its fine appearance and to make it easily absorbable in liquids.

marmalade a preserve, usually based on citrus fruit.

milk
sweetened condensed milk from which 60% of the water has been removed; the remaining milk is then sweetened with sugar.

mixed spice a blend of ground spices usually consisting of cinnamon, allspice and nutmeg.

nutmeg the dried nut of an evergreen tree native to Indonesia; it is available in ground form or you can grate your own with a fine grater.

rolled oats oat groats (oats that have been husked) steamed-softened, flattened, dried and packaged for consumption as a cereal product.

orange blossom water also called orange flower water; a concentrated flavoring made from orange blossoms. Available from Middle-Eastern food stores, some supermarkets and delis. Can't be substituted with citrus flavorings as the is taste completely different.

parchment is a silicone-coated paper that is primarily used for lining baking pans and oven trays so cakes and cookies won't stick, making removal easy.

pastry sheets packaged ready-rolled sheets of frozen puff and shortcrust (sweet and savory) pastry, available from supermarkets.

peanut butter peanuts ground to a paste; available in crunchy and smooth varieties.

peanuts not, in fact, a nut but the pod of a legume; also called ground nut.

peppermint extract is distilled from the essential oils of peppermint leaves. Commonly used in cooking.

rosewater distilled from rose petals, and used in the Middle East, North Africa and India to flavor desserts. Don't confuse with rose essence, which is more concentrated.

sugar
dark brown a moist, dark brown sugar with a rich, distinctive, full flavor coming from natural molasses syrup.

confectioners' also known as powdered sugar; granulated sugar crushed together with a little added cornflour.

light brown an extremely soft, finely granulated sugar retaining molasses for its characteristic color and flavor.

superfine also called finely granulated table sugar or caster sugar.

turbinado a granulated, golden colored sugar with a distinctive rich flavor; often used to sweeten coffee.

white (granulated) also known as crystal sugar; a coarse, granulated table sugar.

treacle a concentrated, refined sugar syrup with a distinctive flavor and dark black color.

wheat germ the germ is where the seed germinates to form the sprout that becomes wheat. It has a nutty flavour and is very oily, causing it to turn rancid quickly, so is usually removed during milling. Available from health-food stores and supermarkets.

INDEX

CONVERSION CHART

measures

All cup and spoon measurements are level. The most accurate way of measuring dry ingredients is to weigh them. When measuring liquids, use a clear glass or plastic measuring cup with metric markings.

We use large eggs.

dry measures

STANDARD	METRIC
½oz	15g
1oz	30g
2oz	60g
3oz	90g
4oz (¼lb)	125g
5oz	155g
6oz	185g
7oz	220g
8oz (½lb)	250g
9oz	280g
10oz	315g
11oz	345g
12oz (¾lb)	375g
13oz	410g
14oz	440g
15oz	470g
16oz (1lb)	500g
24oz (1½lb)	750g
32oz (2lb)	1kg

liquid measures

STANDARD	METRIC
1 fluid oz	30ml
2 fluid oz	60ml
3 fluid oz	100ml
4 fluid oz	125ml
5 fluid oz	150ml
6 fluid oz	190ml
8 fluid oz	250ml
10 fluid oz	300ml
16 fluid oz	500ml
20 fluid oz	600ml
32 fluid oz	1000ml (1 litre)

length measures

STANDARD	METRIC
⅛in	3mm
¼in	6mm
½in	1cm
¾in	2cm
1in	2.5cm
2in	5cm
2½in	6cm
3in	8cm
4in	10cm
5in	13cm
6in	15cm
7in	18cm
8in	20cm
9in	23cm
10in	25cm
11in	28cm
12in (1ft)	30cm

oven temperatures

The oven temperatures in this book are for conventional ovens; if you have a fan-forced oven, decrease the temperature by 10-20 degrees.

	°F (FAHRENHEIT)	°C (CELSIUS)
Very slow	250	120
Slow	300	150
Moderately slow	325	160
Moderate	350	180
Moderately hot	400	200
Hot	425	220
Very hot	475	240

This decadent and luscious book is filled with recipes for indulgent macarons, scrumptious bars and beautiful biscotti. The kitchen cookie jar will always need replenishing as each delicious bite-sized treat is devoured. All the most-loved delights are here: shortbread, chocolate chip cookies, melting moments and caramel bars. Each one is irresistible and perfect for morning or afternoon tea, as a lunchbox snack or as a heavenly after-dinner luxury. Every recipe has been triple-tested so you get great results every time!

BG - Cookbooks
ISBN 978-1-4351-4562-7

Printed in China